*Story time with*

# Proverbs

Part-2

Simmi Anand



BlueRose Publishers

First Published in January 2021
**ISBN: 978-93-5427-372-8**

**BLUEROSE PUBLISHERS**

www.bluerosepublishers.com
info@bluerosepublishers.com
+91 8882 898 898
**Cover Design:**
Shivangi Lohia
**Typographic Design:**
Deepika Matpal
**Distributed by:** BlueRose, Amazon, Flipkart, Shopclues

*Hello kids,*

*I hope all of you enjoyed the first part of this book. I am back with a few more stories and proverbs.*

*Let's revise about proverbs. Proverb is a short saying widely used to express an obvious truth based on common sense or experience. They have deep meaning and are retold through generations.*

*Pia is back with some more interesting proverbs and stories for you. Her parents Dhruv and Maya will be along with her to teach some new things.*

*Let's start learning.*

# CONTENT



Illustrations by- Ankita Agarwal & Kanika Agarwal

Editing by- Anamita Guha

## 1) Better late than never

*It is better for someone to arrive late (or something to happen late) than never to arrive (or never to happen).*

*Pia was sitting in her 'baby seat' inside the car and playing with her toys. She was very excited as they were going to an amusement park that day. She was humming her favourite song.*

*Maya turned back at Pia and smiled. She said, 'You look so happy today. Have you decided which all rides you want to go?'*

*Pia replied in excitement, ' I will go on all the rides. Drive fast, daddy.'*

*Maya and Dhruv were happy to see Pia excited.*

*The car stopped at the red signal.*

*Pia frowned and asked impatiently, 'Why are we stopping so often? When will we reach? The park will close.'*

*Dhruv explained to her, 'We have to follow the traffic rules. There are so many people on the road. Everyone has to reach somewhere. All of us can't move together. We need to give everyone a chance to move towards their* *destination. So, these traffic signals have been <u>installed</u> at regular intervals. You remember what we taught you about traffic colours, right?'*

*Pia replied in a dull voice, 'Yes.'*

*Maya said, 'Let's sing it together. Shall we?'*

*Dhruv continued the song.*

*He said, 'When the light is green, I will go ahead like a queen.*

*When the light is yellow, I will slow down dear fellow.*

*When the light is red, I will stop and won't go ahead.'*

*Pia and Maya also sang together.*

*The song cheered Pia a little. However, they saw someone violating a red signal on the other side of the road.*

*Pia said, 'Look over there. That white car didn't follow the red signal rule. Can we also go?'*

*Maya and Dhruv were shocked at this question. But it wasn't Pia's fault. When adults don't understand the seriousness of the rules and follow them sincerely, how can we expect a five-year-old to understand.*

*When the signal turned green, Dhruv started moving the car ahead.*

*Maya said, 'Dear, these rules are for our safety. We all need to cooperate. If everyone follows these rules, there won't be any accidents. If someone is making a mistake, we should not repeat the mistake. We need to be cautious and cooperative on the roads.'*

*Pia nodded in agreement. She said, 'I understand. We need to be responsible citizens.'*

*Dhruv and Maya clapped for her. Pia was happy. Then they reached another red signal and stopped.*

*A blue car didn't stop at the signal and sped straight ahead on the road. Within a few seconds, it collided with another vehicle coming from the opposite direction. There was a loud bang, followed by the screeching sound of the tyres. Everyone panicked after watching such a gruesome accident. Some rushed to rescue the injured. Some started calling the ambulance and the police. The blue car was upside down and broken. At the same time, the other vehicle was also seriously damaged.*

*Pia got scared and started crying. Maya was in shock too.*

*Maya consoled Pia. She said, 'Calm down. Everything will be fine.'*

*Pia asked, 'What will happen to them now?'*

*Maya replied, 'We don't know. Let the healthcare staff come and attend to them. I hope now you understand what happens when someone does not follow the traffic rules. That guy in the blue car was in a hurry and he violated the rules. He risked not only his life but others too.'*

*Pia sobbed and said, 'Yes, mumma. I understand now.'*

*Maya said, 'See, that guy violated the rules and paid a high price. We will pray that they are safe. It would have been better if he had reached his destination late than meet with this accident and get hurt. So, better late than never.'*

*Pia nodded in agreement and said, 'Now I understand how important it is to follow traffic rules for everyone's safety.'*

***Word meanings:***

*Signal - A movement, action or device giving directions, warnings etc.*

*Frowned - to wrinkle the forehead, to show anger or unhappiness*

*Traffic rules – law guiding people on how to behave on roads while driving, walking etc.*

*Installed – to put something in the correct position.*

*Cautious – to be careful, avoid danger.*

*Cooperative- to help and work together.*

*Screeching – a harsh, shrill sound.*

*Gruesome - extremely shocking, usually dealing with death or injury*

## *Questions –*

1. *Where was Pia sitting inside the car?*
2. *Why was Pia excited?*
3. *Why did Dhruv stop the car?*
4. *What is the 'traffic song'?*
5. *Why should everyone follow the traffic rules?*

## *Fun Activity!*

a) *Circle which of the following is **NOT** a part of car.*

*(i) Tyre (ii) Baby car seat (iii) Horn (iv) Swing*

b) *Circle the colours which do **NOT** belong to traffic lights.*

*(i) Orange (ii) Green (iii) Black (iv) Red*

c) *Circle the two things found inside an amusement park.*

*(i) Factory (ii) Hospital (iii) Rides (iv) Ice-cream shops*

d) *Circle the vehicle which goes to places to help sick people.*

*(i) Bus (ii) Truck (iii) Ambulance (iv) Aeroplane*

## 2) Every drop counts

*It means that even if we save a few drops of water, it will add up to a large quantity. Many drops make an ocean. So, every drop of water is important.*

*Pia was brushing her teeth and she had kept the tap on. The water kept flowing out uselessly. Maya came and closed the tap. She said, 'How many times have I told you not to waste water. Please turn on the tap only when you need the water, like when you are cleaning your tongue or rinsing your mouth. '*

*Pia nodded and said, 'Okay mumma.'*

*Maya replied angrily, 'You must understand how important water is and why we need to conserve it.'*

*Maya thought to herself that it was no use telling Pia the same things repeatedly. She had an idea to make her realise the value of water.*

*Next morning when Pia woke up, she rushed towards the washroom.*

*Maya stopped her and said, 'Wait. There is water disruption today. So you can't use the washroom.'*

*Pia cried and said, 'Please do something mumma. I need to use the washroom.'*

*Maya replied, 'If it is so urgent, then you may. But there is little water so you will get to use the washroom only once.'*

*Pia frowned and went inside.*

*After coming out of the washroom, she went to her mother and said, 'I am hungry. Give me pancakes.'*

*Maya replied, 'Oh. I am afraid that is not possible today.'*

*Pia spoke angrily, 'I had told you last night to make it for me.'*

*Maya said, 'There is no water so I couldn't cook today. We will have to wait until the water supply is back.'*

*Pia asked, 'When will it be back?'*

*Maya replied, 'I don't know. There is water shortage everywhere. That's why I always told you to save water. Anyway, I can give you bread and butter for now.'*

*Pia said, 'Ok fine. Give me some water to drink.'*

*Maya handed her a bottle of water and said, 'Drink wisely. This is the last bottle we have. Even the water filter is empty. Prefer not to eat or drink much until the water supply is back. There is no water in the washroom too.'*

*Now Pia realised the trouble. She panicked and asked, 'So we can't go to the toilet, can't eat or drink till water comes?'*

*Maya shrugged and said, 'Unfortunately, no.'*

*Pia sobbed and said, 'I am so sorry for wasting water. I want it back. I want to drink water as much as I want.'*

Maya was happy that Pia learnt her lesson. She said, 'So now you understand why I asked you to save water. Water is a valuable resource. Fresh, clean water is scarce all over the world.'

Pia asked, 'Why is there a shortage of water?'

Maya answered, 'Although we have many water bodies around us, only a small percentage of water can be used for drinking. The world is highly populated, and every living being needs water for survival. We need it for drinking, cooking, bathing, cleaning our laundry, utensils etc. These are just household needs. There are commercial organisations which utilise lots of water for producing different kinds of goods. All your garments, toys, food items etc. come from such industries. Water shortage is due to excessive consumption of water by humans. Also, a large quantity of water gets wasted because of leaky taps, careless usage etc.'

Pia said, 'I will save water from now.'

Maya said, 'Due to water wastage and climate change, there is water crisis everywhere. All of us together can bring a change and save our future generation from disaster. We need to be careful while using taps, repair faulty taps, use dishwashers and washing machines efficiently. These are just a *few of the measures. We all should start saving water as every drop counts.'*

*Pia nodded and said, 'I understand the importance of every drop of water now.'*

***Word meanings:***

*Waste - to use something carelessly*

*Rinsing - to wash off with water*

*Conserve - to keep safe from loss of something*

*Washroom - bathroom, toilet*

*Disruption- disturb.*

*Scarce - shortage*

*Resource - support, wealth*

*Consumption – usage*

***Questions –***

1. *When should we turn on the tap?*
2. *Where did Pia want to go in the morning?*
3. *What did Pia want to eat?*
4. *Why was Maya not able to cook for Pia?*
5. *Why is there a shortage of water?*

***Fun Activity!***

***Find the opposites of the following words;***

*(a) Useless* *(b) Angry*
*(c) Disruption* *(d) Wisely*
*(e) Fresh* *(f) Shortage*

## 3) Haste makes waste

*It means that we should be careful and patient while doing anything. Doing something in a hurry (haste) might result in wastage (waste) of money, time, effort or health.*

It was Pia's birthday and she was excited about her party as all her friends would be coming. She had come out with her parents to get her cake.

Maya was tensed as it was late, and they needed to reach home before the guests arrived. They were busy the whole day in preparing food and decorating the house.

Dhruv said, 'Please calm down. We won't be late. Moreover, even if we are late, we will call them up and ask them to wait for some time. It's no big deal.'

Maya said, 'How can you be so unaffected by this? It will be embarrassing if guests reach when we are not at home.'

Dhruv replied, 'Because they are also parents. So they will understand the situation. We are about to reach the shop. You call the shopkeeper and ask them to keep our things ready. It will save time.'

Maya nodded and called the shopkeeper.

*Dhruv said, 'This is a busy area, so I will stay in the car with Pia. You go and collect things which we had ordered.'*

*The car stopped, and as Maya was in a hurry, she opened the door of the car without checking sideways. A man who was walking on the footpath beside their car collided with the sudden opening of the door and got injured.*

*Maya got scared and rushed to help him.*

*Dhruv asked Pia to stay in the car and got down to help the man.*

*People nearby also stopped to help the hurt person.*

*Maya was apologising sincerely as the person got injured due to her mistake.*

*The man was in no mood to calm down. He threatened to call the police and started shouting at Maya.*

*Maya was crying now.*

*Dhruv said, 'Please sir, I know you are hurt and in pain. But please try and understand that we did not hurt you intentionally. We are extremely sorry. We will pay for your medical expenses if required.'*

*The man said, 'I can't even begin to imagine what would have happened if the collision would have pushed me towards the main road. Some moving vehicle would just run over me. You would be the reason for my death.'*

*After much pleading, the man finally calmed down and asked for a few thousand rupees as compensation.*

*Dhruv felt that the man was taking undue advantage now. However, since he knew it was their mistake, he agreed to pay him.*

*The man left after receiving the cash.*

*Dhruv and Maya got inside the car again. The incident utterly shook Maya.*

*Pia was sitting in the back seat and she was equally troubled. She asked, 'Mumma, are you fine?'*

*Dhruv calmed her down and said, 'It's okay dear. Everything is fine now. Life is full of both bad and good things. We should learn lessons from such incidents. Thankfully he was not injured badly.'*

*Maya spoke up, 'Today, indeed I learnt a big lesson. No matter what the situation is, we should always have patience and be careful because hurrying matters can only bring problems to ourselves and others. Always remember haste is waste.'*

*Pia said, 'Yes I will always be careful and patient.'*

**Word meanings:**

*Guests- a person visiting another home.*

*Embarrassing- to make someone uncomfortable in a situation*

*Rushed- to act or go quickly*

*Apologising - to say one is sorry*

*Compensation - something, mostly money given to someone for their loss or injury*

*Lesson – an experience that leads to gain of some knowledge*

**Questions –**

1. *Why was Maya tensed?*
2. *Why did Dhruv ask Maya to call the shopkeeper?*
3. *What happened when Maya opened the car door?*
4. *What did the injured man threaten to do?*
5. *How did Dhruv want to help the injured person?*

**Fun Activity!**

**Fill in Blanks with words from the story.**

a) *Pia and her parents came out to get her ___________ .*

b) *They were busy the whole day in preparing _________ and decorating the _________ .*

c) *People nearby stopped to _______ the person.*

d) *The man asked for a few _________ rupees as compensation.*

e) *No matter what the situation is we should always be ___________ and __________ .*

## 4) Don't bite the hand that feeds you.

*It means one should not betray/ discard (bite) the person/ thing (hand) that helps them / is of any use to them (feeds you).*

*Pia had come to her ancestral village to meet her grandparents. It was summer vacation, and she would spend an entire month with them. Houses and roads were all so different there. Her grandparents hugged her as soon as she got out of the car. She was so thrilled to meet them. After having her lunch, she sat on her bed with the toys gifted to her by her grandparents. She was excited to have new toys. Suddenly there was power cut. As it was the summer month, it was hot, and she started to sweat. She asked her parents when somebody will switch on the generator.*

*Dhruv replied, 'Things are different here. We don't have a generator facility in the village. We will have to wait for the power to return.'*

*Pia frowned and said, 'How will I stay in this hot weather?'*

*Maya replied, 'It's okay dear. Slowly your body will adapt to this weather.'*

*As some more time passed, Pia started to get restless.*

Her grandfather was talking to her father about how deforestation has increased the temperature in the past few years.

Pia got curious. She asked them, 'What is deforestation?'

Dhruv replied, 'Deforestation is the permanent removal of trees either to use the wood or use the cleared ground to build buildings and factories.'

Pia asked, 'So how does it affect us?'

Maya replied, 'First, you must understand the benefits of trees. We breathe in a gas called Oxygen and breathe out a gas called Carbon Dioxide. The trees around us take in Carbon dioxide and give us Oxygen. Carbon dioxide is a kind of impurity and is hazardous if present in large quantities. It increases the temperature of the atmosphere, which results in climate change. This makes the earth warmer and melts the snow and causes a rise in sea levels, storms etc. So the existence of trees is essential for us as they take in Carbon dioxide.'

*Dhruv added, 'Trees are a source of food not only for us but also other animals. They provide us with so many fruits. Also, when trees are cut, there is a loss of nutrients in the soil, which affects other small plants. The biggest disadvantage is flooding. The roots of the trees help in water absorption so in their absence water will just flow in any direction. Hence, after heavy rains, there are increased chances of flooding, which results in loss of life and many things.'*

*Pia asked, 'So if trees are so important, then why do people cut them?'*

Dhruv replied, 'There are various reasons for that. Some do it to make buildings such as houses, offices etc. or dam construction. It can also be due to mining, agriculture, cattle breeding. Then sometimes deforestation occurs by natural causes such as hurricanes, fires, floods etc.'

Pia nodded and said, 'I understand how important trees are, and that we should save them. Trees are so helpful.'

Maya said, 'Yes trees are very crucial for our existence. Sometimes humans are short-sighted. We don't realise the value of trees and just destroy them. So now we have to tolerate the effects such as climate change. Everyone should plant as many trees as they can. Trees feed us with Oxygen and provide us with so many things. We should always remember not to bite the hand that feeds us.'

**Word meanings:**

Ancestral – belonging to previous generations.

Generator – a machine that produces electricity or other energy.

Impurity- something not pure. Mixed with something harmful

Hazardous- dangerous.

Hurricanes – a powerful storm with heavy rains.

*Crucial - extremely important as many things depend on it*

*Short-sighted - not thinking enough about how an action will affect the future*

***Questions –***

1. *Where did Pia go to meet her grandparents?*
2. *Why was Pia feeling hot?*
3. *What were Pia's father and grandfather talking about?*
4. *What is deforestation?*
5. *What do the roots of the trees help in?*

***Fun Activity!***

***State whether true or False;***

a) *Pia went to meet her grandparents during winter vacation.*

b) *Pia will spend an entire month with her grandparents.*

c) *Deforestation is the permanent removal of trees*

d) *Humans breathe in Carbon Dioxide and breathe out Oxygen.*

e) *Everyone should plant as many trees as they can.*

## 5) Cleanliness is next to godliness

*Cleanliness means staying clean. It helps in maintaining a healthy body and mind.*

*Pia was having lots of fun at the amusement park. She was enjoying in the park with her parents. They were in the park for three hours.*

*Maya just realised it was lunchtime for Pia. She said, 'Pia, please come now. Have some food and then you can continue playing.'*

*Pia didn't want to come down from the slide. She said, 'No, I am not hungry now. I will eat later.'*

*Dhruv said, 'I am starving. We are going to eat. You play and be safe.'*

*Pia ran down from the slide and said, 'Don't leave me alone.'*

*Dhruv and Maya laughed as little Pia came running towards them. They went to a restaurant. As they entered the restaurant, they were shocked to see the condition of the restaurant.*

*There was a dustbin, but waste was hardly inside, and most of the garbage was thrown outside the bin and was lying on the ground.*

*Pia said, 'This place is so dirty.'*

*Maya replied, 'Yes dear. Some people don't take cleanliness seriously. They don't realise its importance.'*

*They went inside to eat.*

*Pia was getting irritated by the flies buzzing around her. She said, 'There are so many flies here. When will they go?'*

*Dhruv tried to get rid of them, but they were just lingering around.*

*Maya said, 'These flies won't leave. Don't you see the mess outside? We need to eat and get out of here fast. I don't have any other option else I wouldn't have eaten here.'*

*Pia asked, 'Why mumma?'*

*Maya replied, 'Dear, there are so many flies and they are carriers of germs. We might get sick.'*

*Pia was curious now. She asked again, 'What is carrier of germs? How will we get sick?'*

*Dhruv replied, 'The mess you saw outside attracts these flies. They go and sit on that dirty and rotten garbage. In the process, they carry minute germs on their legs. Then they come and sit on our food and transfer the germs to our food. When we eat such germ-laden food, we might get sick.'*

*Pia got scared and said, 'I don't want to eat here.'*

*Dhruv consoled her and said, 'We don't have any other option here so we will have to be careful. We should not let the flies sit on our food.'*

*Pia frowned and said, 'If the flies are so dangerous, then why are people throwing garbage outside the bin?*

*Maya replied, 'Because they are not aware and careful. Everyone needs to take care of our planet. Dustbins are installed at regular intervals, and they should be properly used. Officials need to clear the trash at regular intervals and the citizens need to use it responsibly. Only when everyone is careful, we will be free of such a mess.'*

*Dhruv said, 'On a personal level, we should start by keeping our hands and body clean by taking bath daily. Then we should work on keeping our house clean. On a community level, we should stop littering around. Garbage should be thrown only at designated places. No one should spit or urinate in public places. If everyone follows these cleanliness rules, we will get rid of so many diseases. Staying clean is good for our mental health as well. It also increases our immunity.'*

*Pia said, 'Now I understand how important cleanliness is for us.'*

*Maya added, 'Not only for us. It is important for our country, our planet. So many people die every year from various diseases due to contaminated food and water. If cleanliness is maintained, there will be less burden on healthcare facilities and the people too. Overall this will highly benefit the planet. Always remember cleanliness is next to godliness.'*

## Word meanings:

Slide- a smooth sloping track, down which a person or thing can come down easily.

Cleanliness- being clean, not dirty

Lingering- to stay. To be slow to leave.

Germs- Bacteria or viruses that cause diseases.

Garbage- waste products. Food or other things that are thrown away.

Littering- mess of waste materials. Scattered.

## Questions –

1. For how many hours was Pia enjoying in the amusement park?
2. What was the condition of the restaurant?
3. How do people get sick?
4. How should citizens behave?
5. How does staying clean help us?

## Fun Activity!

Write in 6-8 lines how you keep your house clean. Do you take help from your elders for cleaning your room?

## 6) Honesty is the best policy

*Being honest might seem difficult compared to lying to get out of trouble quickly. But all the problems will be worth it in the end as we will gain love and trust by being honest.*

*It was lunchtime, and Pia was sitting in her classroom and enjoying the delicious toast made by her mother. She was chatting with her friends in between. Miss Priya reminded them not to talk while eating as it's not a good habit. Later, when their lunch was over, the kids were taken to the washroom and the classroom was cleaned.*

*Pia came back to her classroom with her friends. All the kids were settling down, and the teachers were busy preparing for the next session. Pia felt thirsty and she took out her water bottle. By mistake, little water got spilt on the floor. But Pia ignored it and continued drinking the water.*

*Once all the children were seated, the teacher started with the session. The teacher walked inside the classroom while she was teaching to pay individual attention to each kid. When she reached near Pia's desk, she slipped and injured her legs and head. Immediately other staff came in to help Pia's teacher.*

*Now, Pia was scared as she knew her teacher slipped on the water she had spilt on the floor. She felt guilty for her mistake.*

*The teacher was taken to the medical room for first aid as her head was bleeding.*

*The principal entered the classroom and announced, 'Your teacher is injured and is being given first aid. As we suspect a fracture in her leg, she will be shifted to the hospital for a check-up. Would anyone like to tell me how did this happen? Who spilt water on the floor? I won't punish, but I just want to know.'*

*Everyone was silent. Pia wanted to accept her mistake, but she was scared.*

*The principal left the room as no one answered.*

*After reaching home, Pia confided in her mother.*

*Maya said, 'It was a mistake, you didn't do anything intentionally so you will be forgiven. But not accepting your mistake was wrong. What if the principal punishes the whole class for your mistake?'*

*Pia started crying. She sobbed and said, 'I don't want to get punished. I am scared.'*

*Maya consoled her. She said, 'Please don't cry. No one will punish you. We will go and meet the principal tomorrow and apologise to her.'*

*They reached school and went straight to the principal's office. Maya enquired about the teacher's health and came to know that luckily the teacher did not suffer a fracture. She breathed a sigh of relief. She said, 'I have come here to apologise on Pia's behalf. She was the one to spill water, but she was scared to admit it.'*

*Pia was looking down and crying silently.*

*The principal held Pia's hand and said, 'I know you are scared. But as I said yesterday, I won't punish you. I just want my students to be honest. If you had informed housekeeping staff that you had spilt water, someone would have cleaned it, and your teacher would not have hurt herself. You can record a sorry message and send it to your teacher. No one is angry with you. Now go home and relax.'*

*After reaching home, Maya said, 'So how are you feeling now?'*

*Pia replied, 'I feel good now. I will send a card and a sorry message to Miss Priya.'*

*Maya said, 'So you understand now that honesty is not an easy trait. It takes a lot of courage to be honest. Honesty releases fear from the heart and brings peace of mind. It helps you gain the love and trust of the people around you. It also makes you brave. Dishonest people might get happiness initially. But when the truth comes out, no one will love them and trust them ever. Always remember honesty is the best policy.'*

*Pia replied, 'I will always be honest from now on. It does relieve us of our guilt.'*

***Word meanings:***

*Delicious- having great taste*

*Spilt- falling off from a container (mostly liquids)*

*Individual- referring to one-person, single person*

*Guilty – ashamed. Feeling bad for having done something wrong.*

*Confided – to share secrets or personal information*

*Trait - a characteristic belonging to one person*

***Questions –***

1. *What was Pia eating during lunch-time?*
2. *What did the teacher remind them of?*
3. *What did Pia do after returning to the classroom?*
4. *How did Pia's teacher injure herself?*
5. *What did the principal say when Pia apologised to her?*

***Fun Activity!***

***Find out synonyms of the following words from the story.***

| | |
|---|---|
| *(a) Tasty* | *(b) Waterless* |
| *(c) Loose balance* | *(d) Feeling sorry* |
| *(e) Crack inside a bone* | *(f) Loyalty* |

## *Trace & write*

Better late than never

Every drop counts

Haste makes waste

Don't bite the hand that feeds you

Cleanliness is next to godliness

Honesty is the best policy

## ***Colouring activity***

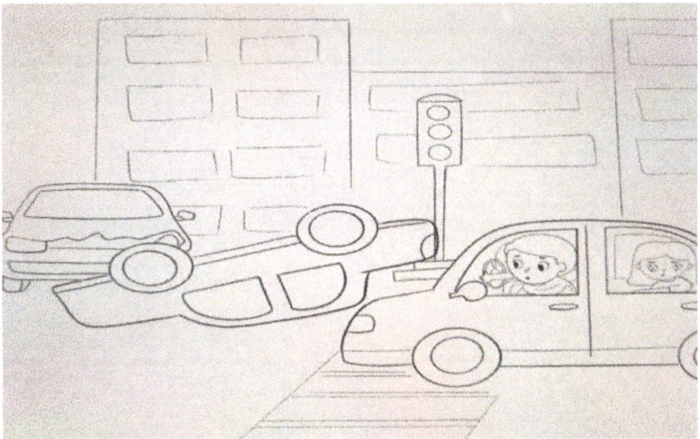

# Other book by author Simmi Anand

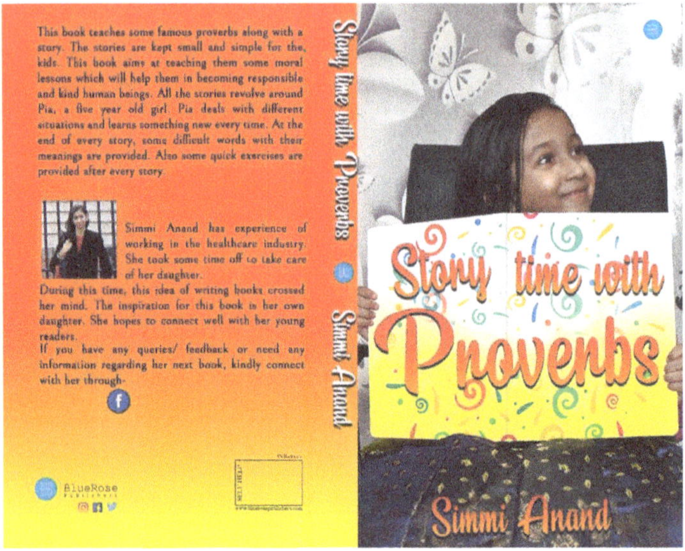


*Available on Blue rose, Amazon and Flipkart.*